7/15

DISCARD

Space

Kay Robertson

rourkeeducationalmedia.com

www.rourkeeducationalmedia.com

PHOTO CREDITS: Cover; © Baris Simsek: © NASA; page 1: © Tim Messick; page 4: © lucentius; page 5: ©NASA; page 6: © Becart; page 8: © Coprid, © NASA; page 11: © NASA; page 13: © rwarnick; pages 14-15: © GeoffBlack; page 16: © Vasko, © kyoshino; page 17: © Dieter Spears; page 19: © rwarnick; page 20-21: © Gunter Hofer; pages 22-23: © knickohr; pages 24-25: © Orla; pages 26-27: © NASA; page 28: © NASA; page 29: © NASA; page 31: © NASA; pages 32-33: © leezsnow; page 34: © Photoeuphoria, © Nicholas Piccillo; page 35: © GlobalP; page 36: © NASA; page 37: © NASA; page 39: © Steve Cole; page 40: © Dieter Spears; page 41: Anatoli Styf; pages 42-43: © monkeybusinessimages; page 44

Edited by: Jill Sherman

Cover and interior design by: Tara Raymo

Library of Congress PCN Data

Also Available as:

STEM Guides to Space / Kay Robertson.
    p. cm. -- (STEM Everyday)
Includes index.
ISBN 978-1-62169-846-3 (hardcover)
ISBN 978-1-62169-741-1 (softcover)
ISBN 978-1-62169-949-1 (e-Book)
Library of Congress Control Number: 2013936451

Rourke Educational Media
Printed in the United States of America,
North Mankato, Minnesota

Rourke
Educational Media

rourkeeducationalmedia.com

customerservice@rourkeeducationalmedia.com • PO Box 643328 Vero Beach, Florida 32964

Table of Contents

Introduction

Have you ever tried to count the stars? It's hard to do. You can count up only so high, but eventually you lose track of where you started. Space, just like the number of stars that fill it, is infinite. It goes on and on... and on!

You can explore space by looking through a telescope!

For as long as human beings have lived, we've been fascinated by the stars and planets. The exciting thing about being alive today is that we have the technology to leave the Earth and explore those other planets.

What we'll find there is a mystery. Maybe we'll meet other forms of life. Maybe we'll find other planets that the human race can colonize. Maybe we'll discover the origins of the universe!

In this book you'll see how math helps scientists to understand space, the size of the solar system, and conditions on other planets. If you're interested in studying outer space, you're going to need to know math. As you will see, math is a large part of what makes space exploration possible!

A Look at the Moon

July 20, 1969 is an important date for the human race. It was on this day that a human being first walked on the surface of the moon.

The Apollo 11 mission that put men on the moon is one of the most extraordinary achievements of the human ra

STEM Fast Fact!

Neil Armstrong

Neil Armstrong was an American astronaut and the first person to walk on the moon. Six hundred million people watched the first moon walk on TV. His footprints can still be seen on the moon today. The dust is thick, but there isn't any wind to remove them. He was awarded the Presidential Medal of Freedom, which is the highest honor a civilian can earn from the U.S. government.

Neil Alden Armstrong
(1930 – 2012)

For years, people watched the moon in the sky and wondered what it was really like. But through careful study the astronauts who went to the moon had a good idea of what to expect.

Planet Earth **revolves** around a much larger body, the Sun. The same pattern follows with the Earth and the moon. Because it is always in motion, the moon is never precisely the same distance from the Earth. When it is closest, the moon is about 227,000 miles (365,321.09 kilometers) from the Earth. When it is farthest away, the moon is about 254,000 miles (408,773.38 kilometers) from the Earth.

Sun

Moon

Earth

Moon's Orbit

Earth's Orbit

Using those figures, you can calculate the average distance from the Earth to the moon.

An average is a number that represents a group of numbers. Calculating the average shows you how far the moon typically is from the Earth.

The moon actually has several looks, or phases.

STEM in Action?

Perhaps your parents give you an allowance for the different chores you do each week. Even though you get a different amount each week, you can calculate your average weekly allowance. Let's say that your allowance for three weeks is:

Week 1 = $12.50

Week 2 = $13.85

Week 3 = $11.20

Based on those numbers, what would your average weekly allowance be?

You can find out in two steps. First, add all the different amounts together:

$12.50 + $13.85 + $11.20 = $37.55

The next step is to divide the result by the number of addends. The addends are the numbers you added together. In this case, there were three addends, $12.50, $13.85, and $11.20:

$37.55 ÷ 3 = $12.51

So now you can say that your average allowance for each of those three weeks is $12.51!

Now try the same thing with the distance from the Earth to the moon:

227,000 + 254,000 = 481,000

481,000 ÷ 2 = 240,500

The average distance between the Earth and the moon is 240,500 miles!

The metric system can be applied to space and space travel in an infinite number of ways. For instance, you learned that the average distance from the Earth to the moon is about 240,500 miles. In the metric system, that distance would be measured in terms of kilometers. Converting miles to kilometers is easy. All you have to do is multiply the number of miles by 1.6. So, how many kilometers are there between the Earth and the moon?

240,500 x 1.6 = 384,800

The moon is roughly 385,000 kilometers from the Earth!

STEM in Action?

Another way to think of the distance from the Earth to the moon is by comparison. Consider the distance between two major American cities. The distance between New York City and Los Angeles is roughly 3,000 miles (4,828.03 kilometers).

How does that compare with the distance from the Earth to the moon?

One way to find out is to subtract the smaller number from the larger number:

$$240,500 - 3,000 = 237,500$$

The distance from the Earth to the moon is 237,500 miles greater than the distance between New York and Los Angeles!

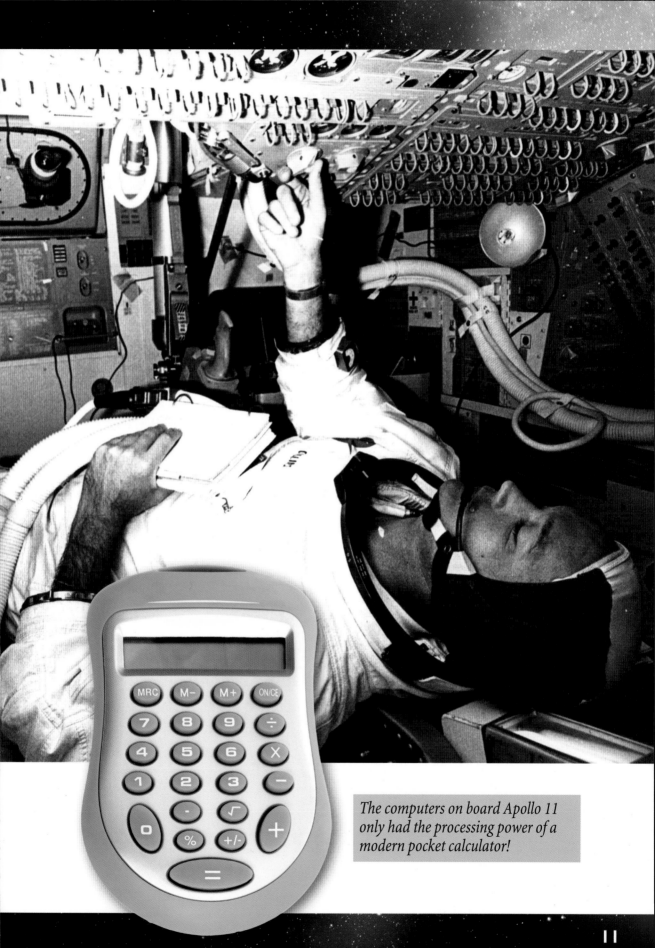

The computers on board Apollo 11 only had the processing power of a modern pocket calculator!

STEM in Action?

You can compare the distance from New York to Los Angeles with the distance from Earth to the moon by using multiples. Any number being multiplied produces multiples. For instance, multiply the number five by some common **integers**:

$$0 \times 5 = 0 \quad 1 \times 5 = 5 \quad 2 \times 5 = 10$$

The answers, 0, 5, and 10, are all multiples of 5! Now consider these numbers:

$$6 \qquad 24$$

What would you have to multiply the number 6 by to give the product 24? You can find out by using division:

$$24 \div 6 = 4$$

Multiplying 6 by 4 gives you 24. Another thing you can say here is that the product 24 is four times as great as six!

Let's do the same thing with the two distances:

$$240,500 \div 3,000 = 80.16$$

The distance from the Earth to the moon is about 80 times as great as the distance from New York to Los Angeles!

Try This

Liftoff!

The Apollo 11 journey began on July 16, 1969. If it took 4 days for the astronauts to cover a distance of 240,500 miles, how fast were they traveling?

First you need to know that there are 24 hours in a day. Now, find out how many hours there are in 4 days:

$$4 \times 24 = 96$$

There are 96 hours in 4 days!

Now divide the distance of the trip by the number of hours:

$$240,500 \div 96 = 2,505.20$$

The astronauts traveled to the moon at a speed of roughly 2,500 miles per hour!

Most of this rocket will not actually travel into space. The bottom portions merely push the space capsule on top out of Earth's field of gravity.

Our Solar System

The Earth is part of a much larger group of planets, all of which **orbit** around the Sun. That is why we call this cluster of planets our solar system.

In our solar system there are eight planets.

Venus

Mercury

Sun

Earth

Mars

Jupiter

Saturn

Uranus

Neptune

Did You Know

Pluto

Pluto was once considered the ninth planet in our solar system. However, in 2006 scientists decided Pluto was too small to be called a planet. They reclassified Pluto as a dwarf planet.

The planet Earth is a big place. It supports a population of more than 7 billion people. But Earth is not the largest planet in the solar system. In order to understand planet sizes, you need to know a little about diameter.

If someone asked you to measure the length of your bed, you could do it by using a tape measure or even a ruler. But what if someone asked you to measure the length of a basketball?

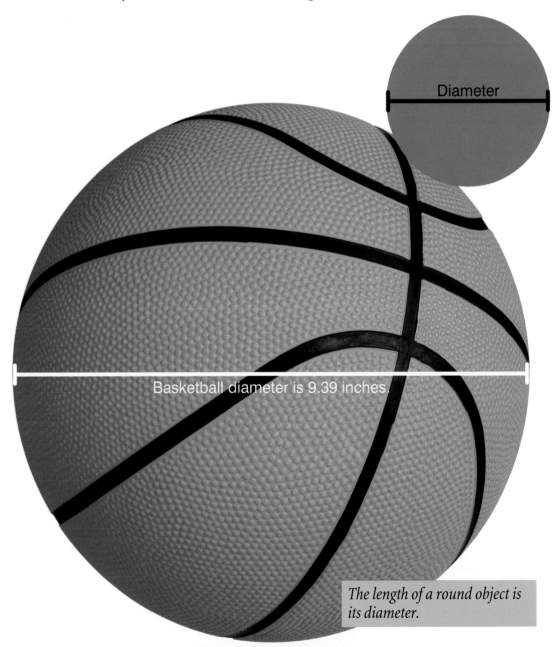

Diameter

Basketball diameter is 9.39 inches.

The length of a round object is its diameter.

A round object is measured somewhat differently than a flat object. Measuring the length of that basketball would be tricky. But measuring something round and flat, like a pizza, wouldn't be too hard. All you would need to do is put a ruler over the pizza and find the distance between two points on the crust. To make sure that you were measuring the longest distance between two points on the pizza, you would make sure that the ruler passed over the center of the pizza.

This is how **diameter** works. The diameter is the distance between two points on the **circumference**, or edge, of a circle and passing through the center of the circle. Diameter is how we measure the size of a planet.

The Earth has a diameter of about 7,927 miles (12,757 kilometers). The moon, by comparison, has a diameter of about 2,160 miles (3,476 kilometers).

To make things easier, let's round off those numbers. We can say that the Earth has a diameter of roughly 8,000 miles (12,874 kilometers) and the moon has a diameter of 2,000 miles (3,218 kilometers).

8,000 miles diameter

STEM in Action ?

How would you compare these two distances? You can subtract the smaller number from the larger number:

$$8,000 - 2,000 = 6,000$$

The Earth's diameter is roughly 6,000 miles greater than the diameter of the moon!

Another way to compare these distances is to use multiples:

$$8,000 \div 2,000 = 4$$

The Earth's diameter is roughly 4 times greater than the diameter of the moon. Or, to put it another way, the moon's diameter is about 1/4 that of the Earth!

2,000 miles diameter

Let's look at the list of planets in our solar system again. This time, though, we're going to include the diameter of each planet:

Mercury – 3,049 miles (21,000 kilometers)
Venus – 7,565 miles (12,174 kilometers)
Earth – 7,927 miles (12,757 kilometers)
Mars – 4,243 miles (6,828 kilometers)
Jupiter – 89,500 miles (144,036 kilometers)
Saturn – 75,000 miles (120,700 kilometers)
Uranus – 32,125 miles (51,700 kilometers)
Neptune – 30,938 miles (49,789 kilometers)

Jupiter is the largest of the eight planets in our solar system.

How much bigger is Jupiter than the Earth?

$$89{,}500 - 7{,}927 = 81{,}573$$

The diameter of Jupiter is about 81,573 miles greater than that of the Earth! Another way to express Jupiter's size would be to use multiples like you did with the Earth and the moon. Just divide the larger number by the smaller number:

$$89{,}500 \div 7{,}927 = 11.29$$

Jupiter is roughly 11 times the size of the Earth!

The number that probably caught your attention is the diameter for Jupiter. As you can see, Jupiter is much larger than the other planets in our solar system.

Diameters of Objects in Our Solar System

Sun
864,000 miles
(1,390,473.22 kilometers)

Mercury
3,049 miles
(21,000 kilometers)

Venus
7,565 miles
(12,174 kilometers)

Earth
7,927 miles
(12,757 kilometers)

Mars
4,243 miles
(6,828 kilometers)

Here's a question. What is the largest object in our solar system?

Maybe you said Jupiter. It seems like the obvious answer, considering Jupiter's massive size. However, there is a much larger object in the solar system.

The Sun!

Compared to the Sun, even gigantic Jupiter looks tiny. The diameter of the Sun is estimated to be about 864,000 miles (1,390,473.22 kilometers)!

STEM in Action ?

How does the Sun's diameter compare with Jupiter?

$$864{,}000 \div 89{,}500 = 9.65$$

We can say two things with this result. First, we can say that the Sun is roughly 10 times the size of Jupiter. We can also say that Jupiter is about one tenth the size of the Sun!

How does the Earth compare with the Sun?

$$864{,}000 \div 7{,}927 = 108.9$$

The Sun is about 109 times the size of the Earth!

Jupiter
89,500 miles
(144,036 kilometers)

Saturn
75,000 miles
(120,700 kilometers)

Uranus
32,125 miles
(51,700 kilometers)

Neptune
30,938 miles
(49,789 kilometers)

STEM Fast Fact!

Satellites

Our solar system also includes a multitude of smaller objects that orbit the eight major planets. These smaller objects are sometimes called **satellites**. The planet Earth has only one satellite, the moon. Other planets have many more. Uranus has 27 satellites. How many more satellites does Uranus have than Earth?

$$27 - 1 = 26$$

Uranus has 26 more satellites than planet Earth!

Measuring Distance

Now that you have looked at the sizes of the different planets and the Sun, you may be wondering how big the entire solar system is. This is a tricky question. It depends on what we consider to be the **boundary** of the solar system. Although some scientists prefer to reach further into space, many have used the location of Pluto, one of the dwarf planets, as the outer edge of our solar system.

The size of Jupiter, even the size of the Sun, is nothing compared to the vast distances between planets. These lengths are so big that scientists even developed a special measurement to deal with them. This measurement is called **astronomical units** (AU). One astronomical unit is the distance from the Sun to the Earth, which is about 92.9 million miles (149.5 million kilometers) or 1 AU.

Our solar system resides in the Milky Way galaxy, which is shaped like a spiral.

Pluto is 39.4 AU from the Sun. Remember that diameter is like a line connecting two opposite points on a circle and passing through the center. So imagine that the distance from the Sun to Pluto is half of a diameter line.

Mercury

Venus

Sun

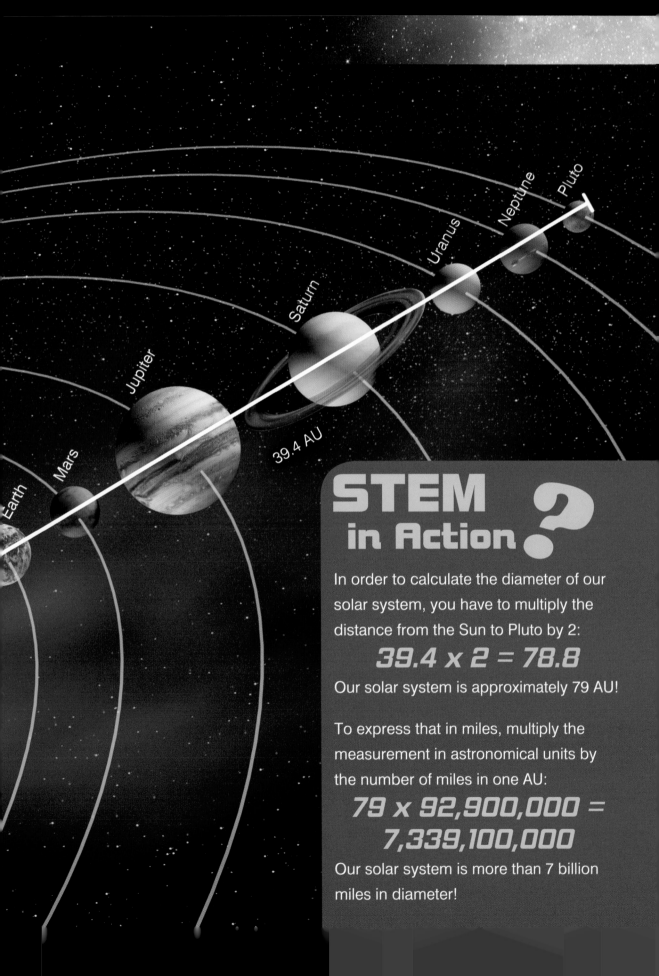

Earth
Mars
Jupiter
Saturn
Uranus
Neptune
Pluto

39.4 AU

STEM in Action ?

In order to calculate the diameter of our solar system, you have to multiply the distance from the Sun to Pluto by 2:

$$39.4 \times 2 = 78.8$$

Our solar system is approximately 79 AU!

To express that in miles, multiply the measurement in astronomical units by the number of miles in one AU:

$$79 \times 92{,}900{,}000 = 7{,}339{,}100{,}000$$

Our solar system is more than 7 billion miles in diameter!

Now that you have some knowledge of astronomical units, you can examine how far other planets are from Earth.

Here is a list of the eight major planets and their distances from the Sun:

Mercury – .04 AU

Venus – .07 AU

Earth – 1 AU

Mars – 1.5 AU

Jupiter – 5.2 AU

Saturn – 9.6 AU

Uranus – 19.2 AU

Neptune – 30.1 AU

STEM Fast Fact!

Mars Rover

Curiosity is a car-sized robotic rover exploring Gale Crater on Mars as part of NASA's Mars Science Laboratory mission.

The main scientific goals of the MSL mission are to help determine whether Mars could ever have supported life, as well as determining the role of water, and to study the climate and geology of Mars.

The surface of Mars appears red because it is composed of rusting iron.

STEM in Action?

If Mars is 1.5 AU from the Sun and Earth is 1 AU from the Sun, how far is Mars from Earth?

$$1.5 - 1 = .5 \text{ AU}$$

Mars is .5 AU from Earth. How many miles is that?

$$92,900,000 \times .5 = 46,450,000$$

Mars is about 46 million miles from Earth!

STEM in Action ?

Earlier, we calculated that the Apollo 11 astronauts traveled to the moon at a speed of 2,500 miles per hour (4,630 kilometers per hour).

How long would it take astronauts to reach Mars at that speed?

$$46,450,000 \div 2,500 = 18,580$$

18,580 hours! How many days is that?

$$18,580 \div 24 = 774.1$$

About 774 days!

If there are 365 days in a year, how many years would it take the astronauts to reach Mars?

$$774 \div 365 = 2.12$$

More than 2 years!

The spacecraft that traveled to the moon in 1969 traveled much more slowly than modern spacecraft. If a mission to Mars was undertaken today it would use ships that could travel at much greater speed. Most scientists imagine a journey time of mere months. Some think the journey could be made in as little as 6 months.

NASA's new spacecraft for human exploration, Orion, is being built for crewed missions to the moon and other deep space destinations like asteroids and Mars. The first manned mission is expected to take place after 2020.

For a crew of astronauts to travel to Mars in just 6 months, how fast would their ship have to go?

Knowing that there are 365 days in a year and that 6 months is half of a year, you can calculate the astronauts' speed.

STEM in Action?

If 6 months is equal to half of one year, how many days is that? You can find out by dividing the number of days in one year by 2:

$$365 \div 2 = 182.5$$

The number of days in 6 months is 183! If there are 24 hours in a day, how many hours are there in 183 days?

$$24 \times 183 = 4,392$$

There are 4,392 hours in 183 days!

To find out the speed that astronauts will have to travel to reach Mars in 6 months, divide the distance (in miles) from Earth to Mars by the number of hours in 6 months:

$$46,450,000 \div 4,392$$
$$= 10,576.04$$

The astronauts would be traveling at roughly 10,600 miles per hour!

STEM
Fast Fact

Light-Years

A unit of measurement closely related to astronomical units is the light-year, also known as the astron.

Light-years are a measurement of the distance traveled by light in a single year, or 365 days. The approximate measure of a light-year is roughly 5.88 trillion miles, or:

5,880,000,000,000 miles!

Light-years are used when measuring distances for which even astronomical units are too small. Just one example is the distance between the Sun and the next closest star in our galaxy, Alpha Centauri. This is a distance of 4.3 light-years.

Can you calculate how many miles that is?

25,284,000,000,000 miles!

All About Gravity

The orbits of the planets are created by the same force that causes a football to fall back to the Earth after it has been kicked high into the air. We call this force **gravity**.

How much do you weigh? Whatever the number is, you probably express your weight in pounds. Did you know that pounds are actually a measurement of force? Pounds are a measure of how much pull gravity has on an object.

If you have ever tried to pick up a heavy object, you know that some things are heavier than others. A textbook is heavier than a birthday card. A rock is heavier than a pine cone.

The reason weight varies is because of mass. Imagine two objects that are about the same size, such as a baseball bat made from wood and a baseball bat made out of plastic. If they are both roughly the same size, then why does the wood bat weigh more than the plastic bat? The answer is that the wooden bat has more mass.

Mass is a word that describes the amount of matter contained in an object. Objects with more mass weigh more because they have more matter for gravity to pull on. This is why a brick weighs more than a piece of wood that is the same size.

When Neil Armstrong and Buzz Aldrin first walked on the moon, they wore space suits that included weighted boots. This was to compensate for the fact that the moon has far less gravitational pull than the Earth. It makes perfect sense if you remember that the moon is about 1/4 the size of planet Earth!

The moon's gravitational pull is roughly 1/6 that of the Earth. If an object weighs 60 pounds on the Earth, how much would it weigh on the moon?

60 pounds

Without their weighted boots, the astronauts who walked on the moon would have floated off into space!

STEM in Action ?

The moon's gravitational pull is 1/6 that on Earth. To find the value of the fraction, you need to divide the numerator by the denominator:

$$1 \div 6 = 0.16$$

So, to find out how much a 60-pound object weighs on the moon, you just need to multiply the weight of the object by 0.16:

$$60 \times 0.16 = 9.6$$

An object that weighs 60 pounds on Earth would weigh about 10 pounds on the moon!

Before you do any calculations, look at the number used to compare the moon's gravitational pull to that of the Earth—1/6. 1/6 is a **fraction**. Fractions are, in a way, a kind of hidden division problem. Fractions are made up of two numbers. The number above the bar is called the **numerator**. The number below the bar is the **denominator**.

10 pounds

In the future, people are sure to visit other planets in our solar system.

STEM Fast Fact!

Each planet has a different size and mass. What kind of weights will people encounter on them?

Here's a chart that you can use to calculate weights on the eight planets in our solar system:

Mercury - 0.4

Venus - 0.9

Earth - 1

Mars - 0.4

Jupiter - 2.5

Saturn - 1.1

Uranus - 0.8

Neptune - 1.2

Suppose a person weighs 150 pounds (68 kilograms) on Earth. How much would that person weigh on Mars?

How much would you weigh on other planets?

150 pounds

Earth

60 pounds

Mars

375 pounds

Jupiter

STEM in Action ?

To find out, you only have to multiply the Earth weight by the number next to the planet you're calculating for:

$$150 \times 0.4 = 60$$

A person who weighs 150 pounds on Earth would weigh about 60 pounds on Mars!

How much would that same person weigh on Jupiter?

$$150 \times 2.5 = 375$$

375 pounds!

The basic unit of mass in the metric system is the kilogram. In order to convert from pounds to kilograms, you must multiply the pound measurement by 0.45. So, if an astronaut weighs 175 pounds on Earth, how many kilograms is that?

$$175 \times 0.45 = 78.75$$

About 79 kilograms!

How many kilograms would that astronaut weigh on Mars?

$$79 \times 0.45 = 35.55$$

An astronaut who weighs roughly 79 kilograms on Earth would weigh about 35 kilograms on Mars!

Think about the moon the next time you watch the tides crash on the beach!

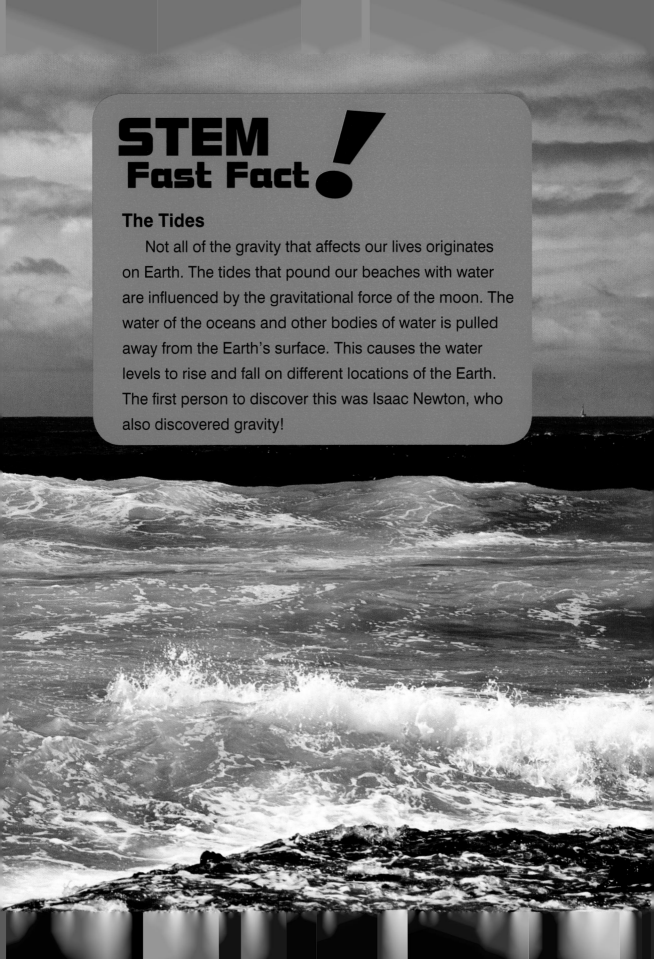

STEM
Fast Fact !

The Tides

Not all of the gravity that affects our lives originates on Earth. The tides that pound our beaches with water are influenced by the gravitational force of the moon. The water of the oceans and other bodies of water is pulled away from the Earth's surface. This causes the water levels to rise and fall on different locations of the Earth. The first person to discover this was Isaac Newton, who also discovered gravity!

Conclusion

Now that you have some knowledge of how space exploration and math are related, you probably have a lot more respect for all the work that goes into a space mission. A lot of hard work and preparation is needed for a safe and successful journey.

Maybe you'll want to consider becoming an astronaut. Maybe you can become an engineer and design space crafts. Dream big, anything is possible!

Study hard and one day

Glossary

astronomical units (ass-truh-NOM-uh-kuhl YOO-nitz): measurements used to chart distances in outer space

boundary (BOUN-duh-ree): the outer limit of something

circumference (sur-KUHM-fur-uhnss): the edge, or outline of a circle

denominator (di-NOM-uh-nay-tur): the bottom number of a fraction

diameter (dye-AM-uh-tur): the length of a straight line passing through the center of a circle

fraction (FRAK-shuhn): another way of writing a division problem; a number composed of two numbers

gravity (GRAV-uh-tee): the invisible force that attracts smaller bodies to a planet

numerator (NOO-muh-ray-tur): the top number of a fraction

orbit (OR-bit): the path of a body in space as it revolves around another, larger body

revolves (ri-VOLVZ): spins; rotates

satellites (SAT-uh-litz): bodies that orbit a planet

Index

Metric System

We actually have two systems of weights and measures in the United States. Quarts, pints, gallons, ounces, and pounds are all units of the U.S. Customary System, also known as the English System.

The other system of measurement, and the only one sanctioned by the United States Government, is the metric system, which is also known as the International System of Units. French scientists developed the metric system in the 1790s. The basic unit of measurement in the metric system is the meter, which is about one ten-millionth the distance from the North Pole to the equator.

Converting Imperial to Metric			
Convert	To	Multiply by	Example
inches (in)	millimeters (mm)	25.40	2in x 25.40 = 50.8mm
inches (in)	centimeters (cm)	2.54	2in x 2.54 = 5.08cm
feet (ft)	meters (m)	0.30	2ft x .30 = 0.6m
yards (yd)	meters (m)	0.91	2yd x .91 = 1.82m
miles (mi)	kilometers (km)	1.61	2mi x 1.61 = 3.22km
miles per hour (mph)	kilometers per hour (km/h)	1.61	2mph x 1.61 = 3.22km/h
ounces (oz)	grams (g)	28.35	2oz x 28.35 = 56.7g
pounds (lb)	kilograms (kg)	0.454	2lb x .454 = 0.908kg
tons (T)	metric ton (MT)	1.016	2T x 1.016 = 2.032
ounces (oz)	milliliters (ml)	29.57	2oz x 29.57 = 59.14ml
pint (pt)	liter (l)	0.55	2pt x .55 = 1.1l
quarts (qt)	liters (l)	0.95	2qt x .95 = 1.9l
gallons (gal)	liters (l)	3.785	2gal x 3.785 = 7.57

Websites to Visit

www.pbs.org/teachersource/mathline/concepts/space.shtm
PBS Teacher Source – Mathline, Space

www.hypertextbook.com/facts/2004/StevenMai.shtml
Hypertextbook – Diameter of the Solar System

library.thinkquest.org/CR0215468/apollo_11.htm
Think Quest – Apollo 11

Show What You Know

1. How far is Earth from the Sun?

2. Define gravity. What happens when astronauts travel to the moon?

    Are they heavier or lighter?

3. How do scientists classify Pluto?

4. Which is the largest planet in the solar system?

5. What is the name of our galaxy?

BLACK FIRE™

HERNÁN RODRÍGUEZ

ARCHAIA ENTERTAINMENT LLC
WWW.ARCHAIA.COM

Troy Peteri, *Lettering*
Anna Rosen Guercio, *Script Translation*
Rebecca Taylor, *Editor*
Scott Newman, *Production Manager*

Archaia Entertainment LLC

PJ Bickett, *CEO*
Mark Smylie, *CCO*
Mike Kennedy, *Publisher*
Stephen Christy, *Editor-in-Chief*

Published by **Archaia**

Archaia Entertainment LLC
1680 Vine Street, Suite 1010
Los Angeles, California, 90028, USA
www.archaia.com

ARCHAIA™
NEW STORIES. NEW WORLDS.

BLACK FIRE Original Graphic Novel Hardcover. November 2011. FIRST PRINTING

10 9 8 7 6 5 4 3 2 1

ISBN: 1-936393-38-7
ISBN 13: 978-1-936393-38-1

Printed in China.

BLACK FIRE™

WRITTEN AND ILLUSTRATED BY
HERNÁN RODRÍGUEZ

BASED ON AN ANONYMOUS MANUSCRIPT
DISCOVERED IN CARCASSONNE.

CLACK!

CRACK!

CRACK!

AAGH!

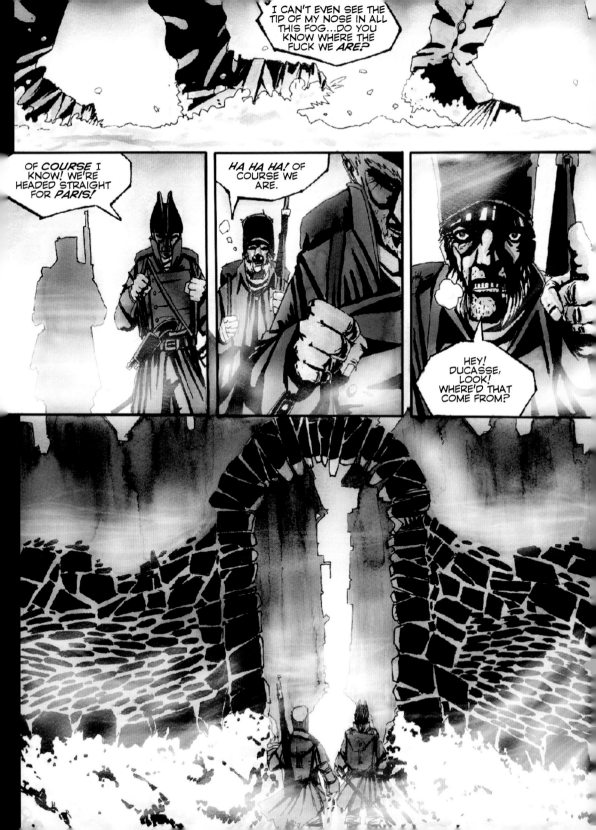

 GLUP! GLUP!

 AHH! I WAS SO THIRSTY!

 I NEVER DREAMED YOU COULD DIE OF THIRST WITH SO MUCH SNOW AROUND, BUT IT'S SO HARD TO KEEP WATER FROM FREEZING! AND IF YOU EAT SNOW YOU WIND UP SPITTING OUT BITS OF LUNG...

 HOW LONG HAVE YOU BEEN IN THIS ABANDONED VILLAGE?

 NOT EVEN A DAY... WE WERE HIDING IN THE CHURCH, BECAUSE IF THE COSSACKS COME THEY MIGHT THINK TWICE ABOUT SETTING A CHURCH ON FIRE.

 WE'RE THE ONLY PEOPLE IN THE VILLAGE? NO ONE ELSE LIVES HERE?

 THAT'S RIGHT...IT'S COMPLETELY ABANDONED.

FOR A LONG TIME NOW! SINCE BEFORE THE WAR...

 HAVE YOU FOUND ANYTHING TO EAT?

 WE SEARCHED THE CHURCH AND THERE'S NOTHING HERE AND NOW IT'S GETTING DARK...

28

THIS COUNTRY NEVER CUTS YOU A BREAK, EVEN WHEN THE SKY IS CLEAR, THE GLARE OFF THE SNOW WOULDN'T LET US SEE...

WE COULDN'T EVEN SEE THE ROAD WE WERE FOLLOWING BECAUSE WE HAD TO COVER OUR EYES...

OUR GUIDE WAS LEFT BLIND AFTER JUST ONE DAY...

AT THE END OF OUR JOURNEY WE WERE COMPLETELY LOST...THE ROAD WAS SHROUDED IN SNOW AND THERE WAS NO SIGN OF IT, NOR ANY VILLAGE OR CITY...

MOST OF US DIED FROM THE COLD, SICKNESS AND HUNGER... OUT OF OUR GROUP OF TWO HUNDRED STRAGGLERS, WE'RE THE ONLY ONES TO REACH THIS FORGOTTEN VILLAGE...

NO, I WAS THE FIRST TO ARRIVE... I'VE BEEN HERE TWO DAYS.

ALL OF YOU ARRIVED TOGETHER?

AND WHO ARE YOU?

MY NAME IS JOAQUIM DO SANTOS...

I'M THE LAST SURVIVOR OF THE THIRTIETH INFANTRY BRIGADE OF THE PORTUGUESE ARMY.

I NEVER MADE IT TO MOSCOW. I WAS INJURED IN THE BATTLE OF BORODINO AND LEFT BEHIND... BY THE TIME I COULD WALK AGAIN, THE RETREAT WAS ALREADY UNDER WAY.

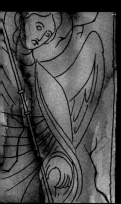

I HEAR SOMEONE CRYING...I THINK IT'S COMING FROM BACK THERE! ARE YOU SURE WE'RE THE ONLY ONES IN THE VILLAGE?

IT'S A SICK YOUNG SOLDIER. HE HAS A FEVER AND WON'T LAST THE NIGHT...

I DON'T KNOW HOW HE MANAGED TO MAKE IT HERE...WE QUARANTINED HIM SO WE WOULDN'T GET SICK...

I HAD A DREAM...

MY BODY CHANGED SHAPE...

WHAT DID YOU CHANGE INTO?

I WAS A RARE TYPE OF INSECT...OR REPTILE...OR BOTH AT ONCE...

MY SKIN WAS TRANSPARENT AND I COULD SEE MY INSIDES...

...AND MY INSIDES SHONE...

AN ANGEL VISITED ME LAST NIGHT... IT SAID IT'D COME FOR ME TODAY...THAT IT'D TAKE ME TO SEE GOD.

AN ANGEL?

GO NOW. I WANT TO DIE ALONE.

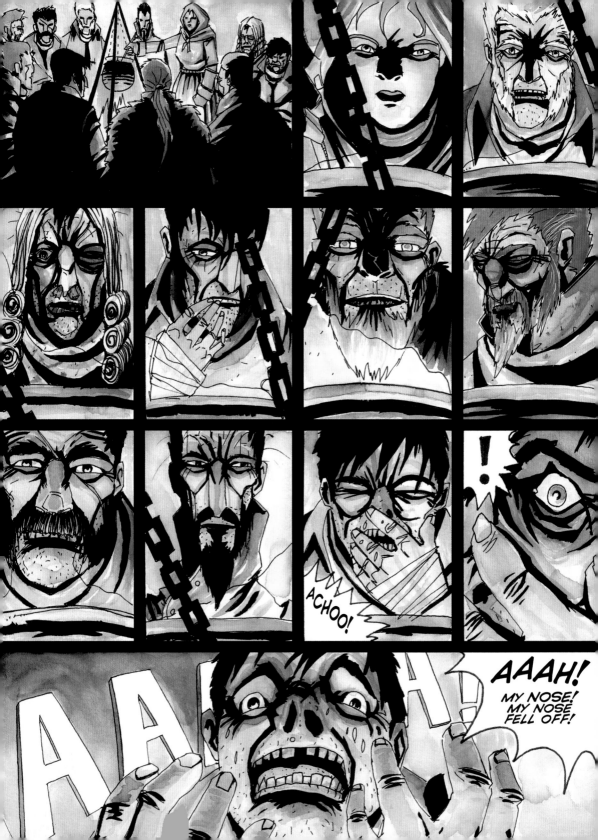

OH NO! NOT MY NOSE!

SHUT UP, YOU IDIOT. WE'VE ALL LOST THINGS FROM THE COLD.

I LOST TWO FINGERS ON ONE HAND...

I'VE LOST PRACTICALLY ALL MY TOES...

TESTA DI CAZZO!

I LOST AN EAR.

AND I LOST FOUR FINGERS!

I LOST MY BALLS.

WHAAAT?

EARLY IN THE RETREAT I HAD REALLY BAD DIARRHEA AND BECAUSE I WAS SHITTING SO MUCH IN THIS INFERNAL COLD, MY BALLS TURNED PURPLE AND THEY HURT REALLY BAD...THEN THEY TURNED BLACK AND STOPPED HURTING... ONE DAY I FOUND THEM...

INSIDE ONE OF MY BOOTS...

THE WORST PART WAS THAT INSTEAD OF CRYING, ALL I COULD DO WAS LAUGH!

HA HA HA HA HA HA HA HA HA HA

NEVER DIG A
HOLE IN THE
SHADE OF A
HANGING MAN
OR THE DARK
GOD YOU
WILL FIND.

DEEP.
SO DEEP.
CZERNOBOG
SLEEPS
WITHOUT
DREAMS.

BETRAYED
BY PERUN,
HE AWAITS
THE DAY HE'S
FREED FROM
HIS PRISON
OF FLESH AND
GOLD.

THE TRAGEDY OF
LIVING DEATH
WILL NEVER END!

WHAT THE HELL WAS THAT? WAS IT THE DYING SOLDIER?

OH GOD! WE'RE GOING TO DIE!

THIS I-IS *IMPOSSIBLE*... THIS MORNING HE WAS DEAD!

HE'S COME BACK TO GET REVENGE ON US FOR LETTING HIM DIE!

HE DIDN'T DIE FROM COLD OR SICKNESS... HE WAS *MURDERED!*

WHAT? EXPLAIN YOURSELF...

TODAY WE FOUND THE POOR DEVIL TORN TO SHREDS... SOMEBODY HAD MURDERED HIM.

DANIEL RAN OFF! WE HAVE TO GO LOOK FOR HIM!

DANIEL IS AN IDIOT AND I DON'T THINK HE'S COMING BACK. IF YOU WANT TO GO LOOK FOR HIM IN THIS STORY, YOU CAN GO ALONE!

WHO DID IT? WHY DIDN'T YOU SAY ANYTHING?

HEY, TAKE IT EASY...

WE DIDN'T WANT TO SAY ANYTHING BECAUSE WE DIDN'T KNOW WHO COULD DO SOMETHING SO HEINOUS, AND, GIVEN THE STATE OF THINGS, ANYONE COULD HAVE GOTTEN BLAMED AND LYNCHED... MAYBE IT WAS ONE OF US, MAYBE IT WAS SOMEONE WE DON'T KNOW WHO'S HIDING IN TOWN...

JUNOT, NO!

IT MUST HAVE BEEN THIS FUCKING PORTUGUESE SON OF A BITCH. YES, YOU, I'VE SEEN HOW YOU LOOK AT JULIE!

I DIDN'T KILL THAT POOR MAN! THE ALBINO WAS THE LAST ONE IN...

ENOUGH ALREADY! CAN'T YOU SEE WHAT I'M TELLING YOU, YOU BUNCH OF JACKASSES? YOU'RE LOOKING FOR ANY EXCUSE TO MASSACRE EACH OTHER.

HOW DID THEY KILL HIM?

WE'RE DOOMED. THIS IS THE END!

WHOEVER DID IT MUTILATED HIM, PUT OUT HIS EYES, HIS NOSE, AND, FINALLY, RIPPED OUT HIS HEART AND HIS LIVER... I'VE NEVER SEEN

FREDERIC, BARRAU, MASSIMO, YOU THREE KEEP WATCH HERE. ORGANIZE SHIFTS. YOU FIRST...DON'T LET THE FIRE GO OUT!

HO CAPITO.

WHAT DIRECTION SHOULD WE TAKE?

GOOD QUESTION...

I'M SURE THIS WAS A MINING TOWN. FROM THE TOWER I SAW A ROAD THAT GOES THROUGH THE MOUNTAINS TO THE WEST.

I'M SURE THAT'S THE ROAD THAT COULD LEAD US OUT OF THIS PLACE.

BUT MAYBE THERE'S NO SUCH ROAD, AND I DON'T LIKE THE IDEA OF GETTING LOST IN THE MOUNTAINS WITHOUT FOOD IN THIS COLD... OR WORSE, THE ROAD COULD BE FULL OF COSSACKS!

THERE ARE NO EASY ROADS TOWARD FRANCE.

TRUE. I'D PREFER TO TAKE MY CHANCES WITH A LEGION OF SAVAGE COSSACKS THAN FACE CZERNOBOG AND HIS UPYRI. THAT WASN'T THE FIRST GHOST I'VE SEEN IN THIS VILLAGE. WHEN WE WENT TO LOOK FOR FOOD I RAN INTO ANOTHER THAT DELIVERED A SIMILAR WARNING BEFORE DISAPPEARING... I THOUGHT I'D GONE CRAZY, BUT NOW I SEE I'M NOT.

SLURP!

BARRAU, YOU'RE SUPPOSED TO BE ON GUARD BY THE FIRE... WHAT ARE YOU DOING ALL ALONE IN HERE?

ALONE?

YOU'RE EATING DAN'S SEVERED HAND? YOU GODDAMN DEGENERATE...

DEPRAVED DWARF!

AAA!

I KNEW IT WAS YOU...

BUUAAAA!

WAM!

WAM!

...WHO KILLED MY HORSE!

I'LL SKIN YOU LIKE A PIG!

COME ON ALREADY, JUNOT! THERE'S NOTHING HERE...

GIVE ME A MINUTE. I'M PRACTICALLY DONE... THIS ROOM'S NEVER BEEN LOOTED. MAYBE THERE'S SOMETHING USEFUL HERE...

I THINK SOMEONE WAS WATCHING WHEN WE SPLIT OFF FROM THE OTHERS...

I DON'T LIKE THIS. WE'RE GOING BACK NOW OR I SWEAR I'LL SHOOT YOU...

ONE SECOND AND WE'LL...HA! THERE IS A GOD! I DON'T CARE WHAT THEY SAY! IF THIS ISN'T FROZEN IT CAN ONLY MEAN ONE THING...

LIQUOR!

GWP! GWP! GWP!

AAAHHH! SWEET NECTAR, HOW IT BURNS! I'D NEARLY FORGOTTEN YOUR LUSCIOUS FLAVOR. WANT A SWIG, JULIE?

JULIE?

THIS PLACE IS ENORMOUS!

AND IT'S FILLED WITH CORPSES... MAYBE THEY THOUGHT THEY'D BE SAFE HERE...

THEY WERE KILLED A LONG TIME AGO...IN THE SAME WAY AT THE SAME TIME...

WOMEN, CHILDREN, THE ENTIRE VILLAGE MASSACRED... MY GOD...

THIS IS A NIGHT-MARE...

BROOM!

WHAT THE HELL WAS THAT?

LOOK! THERE'S ANOTHER DOOR WITH THE SAME SYMBOL...LET'S SEE WHAT'S ON THE OTHER SIDE.

THIS BOOK MUST BE THE CHURCH REGISTER OR ANNALS...

THERE'S ANOTHER PASSAGE-WAY...

QUIET, SOMETHING'S COMING...

115

OUCH!

"CRACKS IN THE NIGHT, THAT'S WHAT THEY CALL THE MOUNTAINS THAT RISE TO THE WEST. THEY SAY THAT BETWEEN THEIR PEAKS THERE ARE VALLEYS SO DEEP THAT NEITHER THE SUN NOR MOON CAN PENETRATE THEM. THEIR NAME IS ANCIENT, IT WAS ONCE USED BY THE NOMADIC NORTHERN TRIBES."

THIS IS SO SHARP...

THE JOURNAL GOES ON ABOUT THE VILLAGE, THE REGION, IRRELEVANT DETAILS...

SIX YEARS AFTER HE ARRIVES, SOMETHING VERY STRANGE HAPPENS...HE SAYS:

"THE SMOKE IS SO HEAVY AND THICK WE CAN'T RESCUE THE MINERS. I PRAY THAT GOD WILL HAVE MERCY ON THEM."

"SOMETHING TRAGIC HAPPENED TODAY. A MINING ACCIDENT, SOME KIND OF COLLAPSE, LEFT MANY OF THE MINERS INJURED AND A DOZEN MISSING. A PUTRID, BLACK SMOKE IS POURING OUT OF THE MINE AND THE CRACKS IN THE MOUNTAIN."

"YESTERDAY I WENT TO GIVE THE LAST RITES TO THE SOLE SURVIVOR. HIS BODY WAS BROKEN BEYOND REPAIR."

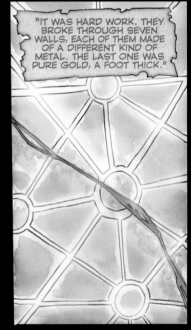

"BEFORE HE DIED, HE TOLD ME SOME OF WHAT WENT ON IN THE DEPTHS OF THAT MINE."

"THE MINERS HAVE BEEN TRAPPED FOR THREE DAYS. WE'VE ONLY MANAGED TO SAVE ONE. THE CAUSE OF THE ACCIDENT IS STILL A MYSTERY. WHEN I ASK ABOUT THE NATURE OF THIS AWFUL EVENT, THE OWNERS OF THE MINE EVADE MY QUESTIONS."

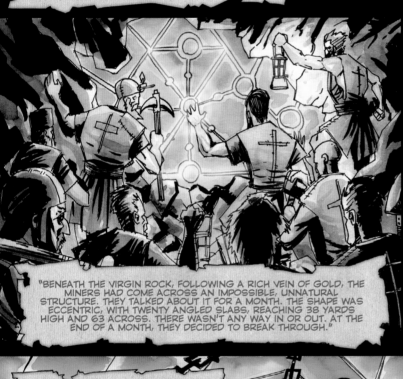

"IT WAS HARD WORK. THEY BROKE THROUGH SEVEN WALLS, EACH OF THEM MADE OF A DIFFERENT KIND OF METAL. THE LAST ONE WAS PURE GOLD, A FOOT THICK."

"BENEATH THE VIRGIN ROCK, FOLLOWING A RICH VEIN OF GOLD, THE MINERS HAD COME ACROSS AN IMPOSSIBLE, UNNATURAL STRUCTURE. THEY TALKED ABOUT IT FOR A MONTH. THE SHAPE WAS ECCENTRIC, WITH TWENTY ANGLED SLABS, REACHING 38 YARDS HIGH AND 63 ACROSS. THERE WASN'T ANY WAY IN OR OUT. AT THE END OF A MONTH, THEY DECIDED TO BREAK THROUGH."

"INSIDE, THEY FOUND A CHAMBER WITH NO WAY IN OR OUT. AS TO WHAT HAPPENED INSIDE, THE MINER COULD ONLY DESCRIBE IT IN THE MOST ENIGMATIC WAY."

"THEY WERE THE LAST WORDS HE SPOKE IN THIS WORLD."

INSIDE THERE WAS A G-GOD... A GOD.

"IT'S BEEN TWO WEEKS SINCE THE ACCIDENT AND WE COULDN'T MANAGE TO SAVE ANYONE ELSE. TODAY THE WIFE OF ONE OF THE MISSING MINERS CAME TO SEE ME."

"SHE TOLD ME THAT HER HUSBAND HAD COME HOME THE NIGHT BEFORE, AS IF NOTHING HAD HAPPENED."

"BUT HE WASN'T THE SAME AS BEFORE, HE BEGAN SAYING HORRIBLE THINGS AND DOING IMPOSSIBLY GROTESQUE THINGS WITH HIS BODY. THEN HE DISAPPEARED INTO THE NIGHT, CARRYING OFF ONE OF HER CHILDREN."

"AT FIRST I THOUGHT THE WOMAN HAD LOST HER MIND WITH GRIEF OVER THE DEATH OF HER HUSBAND."

"BUT SHE WASN'T THE ONLY ONE IN THE VILLAGE THIS SORT OF THING HAD HAPPENED TO."

"AS THE FALL WORE ON, MORE PEOPLE BEGAN TO DISAPPEAR AND THEN SHOW UP AGAIN."

"BUT THEY'D CHANGED."

"TODAY I FOUND THE BODY OF A PASTOR WHO'D BEEN HORRIBLY MUTILATED SOME DAYS BEFORE. HIS HEART AND HIS LIVER WERE MISSING."

"BUT ANOTHER PASTOR SWEARS BY THE CROSS THAT HE SAT UP WITH THE MAN BY THE FIRE LAST NIGHT. LAUGHING, THE MAN TOLD HIM THAT THE ENTIRE VILLAGE WAS GOING TO DIE."

BUT IT DOESN'T END THERE. THERE ARE TESTIMONIALS FROM PEOPLE WHO SWEAR THAT THE "GHOSTS" DIDN'T COME ALONE. SOME CASES TALK ABOUT A SINISTER CHARACTER COVERED IN CHAINS AND ACCOMPANIED BY A HEADLESS WOLF.

IT GOES ON TO LIST SIMILAR CASES, DISAPPEARANCES AND DEATHS. ALL OF THEM HAPPENED THE SAME WAY AND THERE WERE MORE AND MORE. SOME DAYS THEY'D FIND ENTIRE FAMILIES MURDERED...

A WOODSMAN TESTIFIES THAT HE SAW A COLUMN OF BLACK SMOKE AGAINST THE HORIZON IN THE LIGHT OF DAY.

HE SAID HE GOT CLOSER AND SAW THAT INSIDE THE COLUMN THERE WAS A HUMAN SILHOUETTE STRIDING TOWARD THE MOUNTAINS.

BLACK FIRE.

"BUT THERE WAS A MAN CALLED *BOGATYR*, THE FIRST BORN OF DARKNESS, WITH ALABASTER SKIN, KING OF THE TRIBE OF MEN. HE DECIDED TO STOP *CZERNOBOG*, BUT HE DIDN'T CONFRONT HIM ALONE. *KING BOGATYR* FORGED POWERFUL ALLIANCES WITH *LESI*, A WOLF-SPIRIT OF THE FOREST, AND *PERUN*, THE GOD OF THUNDER. TOGETHER THEY LAID A TRAP FOR THE DARK GOD."

"THEY IMPRISONED CZERNOBOG IN THE WORST OF ALL POSSIBLE CAGES FOR AN IMMORTAL: *FLESH*. OUR KING WAS SACRIFICED. IT WAS HIS BODY, HIS BLOOD, THAT CHAINED CZERNOBOG. TRAPPED IN HIS BODY, THE GOD WAS MADE VULNERABLE."

"WITH CZERNOBOG UNABLE TO CHANGE FORM AND SUFFERING THE TRIALS OF THE LIVING, HIS BROTHER, PERUN, BURIED HIM IN THE DEEPEST DEPTHS OF THESE MOUNTAINS."

THOSE POOR PEOPLE, SHUTTING THEMSELVES IN LIKE THAT JUST DELAYED THE INEVITABLE. WE CAN'T MAKE THE SAME MISTAKE. WE HAVE TO GET OUT OF HERE RIGHT NOW.

YES, BUT WHERE DO WE GO? THE END OF THIS BOOK IS ALL ROTTED. IT'S ILLEGIBLE.

WE GET AS FAR AWAY AS POSSIBLE. OR DO YOU NOT GET IT...

HE DOESN'T JUST KILL YOU. HE ENSLAVES YOU SOUL! WHEN HE'S FINISHED, YOU BELONG TO HIM COMPLETELY... HE CONSUMES YOUR SPIRIT TILL YOU'RE NOTHING BUT A SHADOW...

THE ONLY WAY TO GO ON FIGHTING HIM WAS TO EXIST BETWEEN WORLDS, OUT OF HIS REACH. HE POSSESSED SERPIERRE SO THAT HE COULD VANQUISH THE BEAST, ONE OF CZERNOBOG'S MOST POWERFUL SUBJECTS! THE DARK GOD NEVER SAW IT COMING. SADLY, THE PRIEST HAD TO DESTROY HIMSELF TO DO IT.

NOW I SEE...

THE ALBINO IS RIGHT... THE PRIEST REALIZED IN THE END THAT IF HE DIDN'T WANT TO END UP AS ONE OF CZERNOBOG'S SLAVES, HE'D HAVE TO KILL HIMSELF AND BECOME A WANDERING SPIRIT.

HE GUIDED US HERE... HE WANTED US TO FIND THIS ROOM AND LEARN WHAT HAPPENED...

YOU'RE RIGHT, BUT I HAVE THE FEELING THERE'S STILL SOMETHING WE'RE NOT GETTING...OF EVERYONE HERE, WHY ARE WE THE ONLY ONES HE CHOSE TO HELP?

REGARDLESS, WE HAVE TO GET OUT OF HERE AS SOON AS POSSIBLE OR ELSE HIS SACRIFICE WILL HAVE BEEN FOR NOTHING.

126

ARE YOU OKAY? LET ME SEE...

I'M OKAY... IT'S NOT AS BAD AS IT LOOKS... IT COULD HAVE KILLED ME...

I WAS RIGHT. THE LIGHT OF THE SUN DESTROYED IT!

WHERE'D THAT THING COME FROM?

I THINK IT'S MADE FROM THE REMAINS OF THE HORSE AND THE REST OF OUR GROUP...

ONE OF CZERNOBOG'S RUSES TO SLOW US DOWN...

WELL, HE SUCCEEDED. I DON'T THINK I CAN WALK VERY FAST NOW, MUCH LESS CLIMB. DAMN IT!

IT LOOKS LIKE THE DEAD PRIEST ISN'T OUR ONLY ALLY. THE SUNLIGHT IS, TOO... PERUN IS WITH US...

THERE'S THE ROAD!

ON THE THIRD DAY, A GOLDEN LIGHT FILLED MY SOUL AND GOD SPOKE! HE SAID, "THE DEMIURGE HAS FORCED YOU INTO THIS UNCLEAN BODY. TO FREE YOURSELF FROM HIM, FOLLOW THE PATH OF THE TRUE MESSIAH."

WHEN I REACHED THIS HALLOWED GROUND, THE BLACK FIRE ENVELOPED MY BEING AND BURNED AWAY ALL MY SINS AND IMPURITIES... AT LAST THE TRUTH HAS BEEN REVEALED TO ME!

YOU CRAZY FUCKER, I'M GOING TO KILL YOU!

GET READY, SHACKEN...

TODAY I SET OFF DOWN THE PATH OF TRANS-FORMATION! SOON I WILL SIT AT HIS RIGHT HAND!

I AM HIS FIRST APOSTLE AND YOU ARE MY OFFERINGS TO THE ABYSS...

YOU WILL BE CONSUMED BY BLACK FIRE!

THE MOUNTAINS END OVER THERE AND THE STEPPE BEGINS... WE'RE ALMOST THERE...

THAT'S WHERE HIS TERRITORY ENDS...

THIS STRANGE DAGGER WAS IN THE PRIEST'S HAND WHEN HE DIED...THE SYMBOL OF PERUN WILL REPEL CZERNO-BOG.

WHAT ARE YOU DOING?

YOU MUST BE CRAZY! THAT SCAR WILL LAST FOREVER!

THE PRIEST MUST HAVE HAD A GOOD REASON FOR USING IT... I HAVE TO TRUST MY GUTS...

YOU KNOW WE'LL HAVE TO FACE HIM BEFORE WE CAN GET OUT... ONE OF US IS THE SOUL-KEY THAT HE NEEDS TO ESCAPE HIS PRISON... WE CAN'T LET THAT HAPPEN!

ANYONE ELSE?

NO THANKS.

I DON'T THINK IT'LL HELP ANYTHING. THE PRIEST WOUND UP WORM FOOD ANYWAY...

AT LEAST TAKE IT, DUCASSE. IT'S VERY SPECIAL.

I'LL KEEP IT CLOSE AT HAND.

WHAT ODD METAL. IT'S HOT AND COLD AT THE SAME TIME... I'VE NEVER SEEN ANYTHING LIKE IT.

LET'S GET MOVING! THE WOMEN OF FRANCE ARE WAITING FOR ME!

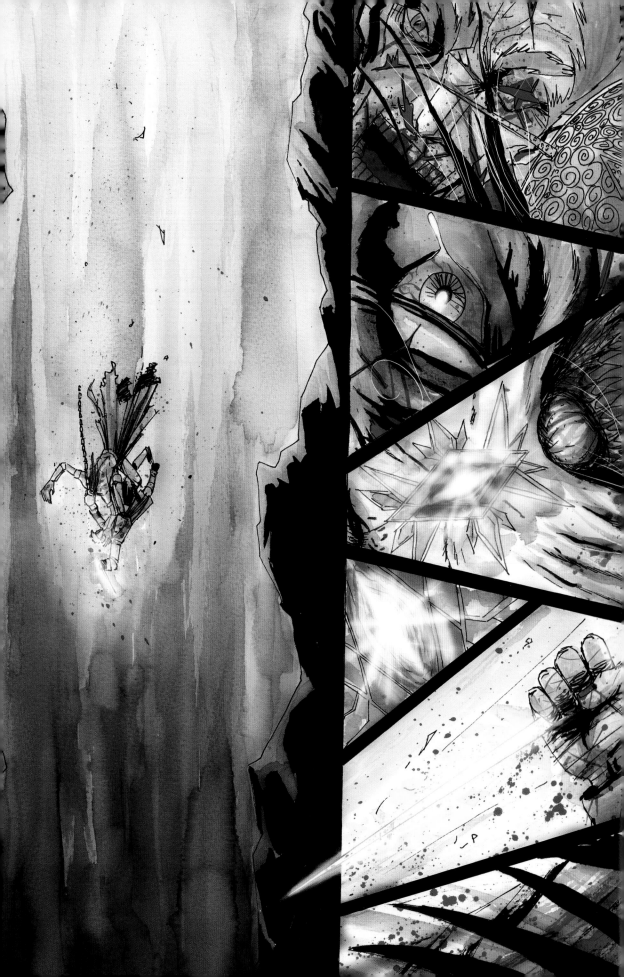

ABOUT THE AUTHOR

HERNÁN RODRÍGUEZ was born in Buenos Aires, Argentina, in 1980. He is the author of *Visions*, two graphic novel adaptations of the works of HP Lovecraft published by Norma Editorial in Spain.